THE BOOK OF
UNITED STATES NAVY SHIPS

THE BOOK OF
UNITED STATES NAVY SHIPS

By M. D. Van Orden
CAPTAIN, U.S. NAVY

ILLUSTRATED WITH PHOTOGRAPHS

DODD, MEAD & COMPANY · NEW YORK

CREDITS FOR PHOTOGRAPHS

Photograph on page 12 is by LTJG B. F. Marrou, U.S.N.R.
All other photographs are official U.S. Navy photographs.

To my grandson, Stanton Sears Coerr
who may some day sail aboard ships of the United States Navy

FOREWORD

In this age of supersonic aircraft and manned flights into outer space, it is well for us to sustain a down-to-earth understanding that three-quarters of our planet's surface is covered by water—and that it is the U.S. Navy which must protect our country's interests in the expansive reaches of the world's oceans.

To meet these responsibilities, the Navy has more than 900 ships, ranging from attack aircraft carriers to wooden-hulled minesweepers. Large or small, each ship is a vital part of the overall Navy team.

The story of the Navy is one of ships and aircraft, but it is also the story of brave men and women whose technical skills, dedication and hard work over the years have made our Navy what it is today. The Navy's tradition of victory is a heritage of which Americans are justifiably proud—for it is Americans who have made it possible.

The challenges of the future are even more exciting and wide-ranging than those of the past. The nuclear age and advanced technology promise adventure of unparalleled scope to those with the courage to seek it out. The Navy accepts its share of this challenge with enthusiasm.

T. H. MOORER
Admiral, U.S. Navy
Chief of Naval Operations

PREFACE

A modern navy is many things—ships, men, aircraft, guns, missiles, equipment, shore bases, machinery, and vehicles of all types—but the heart of any navy is its ships.

Ships are built to many different designs. There may be a number of different types, classes, conversions, and modifications of the basic design. Evolutionary changes occur naturally as normal improvements are made. Sudden drastic changes may be made to adapt to new techniques of warfare or to new technological advances. The change from sail to steam, from wooden hulls to steel; the advent of nuclear power; the shift from guns to missiles—all of these changes resulted in major alterations in ship designs.

The purpose of this book is to present the most important and most representative types and classes of ships in today's United States Navy, and to describe some of their characteristics. In addition, it will discuss the part each ship plays—its "mission"—as a member of the Navy teams—"task forces" and "fleets."

Upon these ships and these teams rest our country's power, prestige, and safety—a strong Navy of strong ships can do much to discourage aggression and preserve the peace.

Washington, D.C.

M. D. Van Orden
Captain, U.S. Navy

CONTENTS

The U.S.S. *New Jersey* (BB-62) alongside the U.S.S. *Crockett* (PG-88).

NAVY TERMINOLOGY

When Navymen talk of their ships, they use words and phrases which may seem strange to those who are not acquainted with the ways of the sea. Yet to seamen those words and phrases have meanings which are well known and precise. They have been developed over many years by seafaring men who chose carefully those expressions which would not be misunderstood by other seamen—even during the stresses of battles or raging storms. Many expressions used today are only representative of past traditions of the sea, yet they are cherished and perpetuated by men who are bound together by their common heritage of service at sea.

Ships are always referred to as "she." There have been many reasons given for this. Some think it is because of the feminine beauty a sailor sees in his ship; others say it is because of the difficulty men have in understanding, directing, and controlling "her." Perhaps the ancient Greeks started the custom by giving their ships female names to honor Athena, the goddess of warships. Whatever the reason, a sailor always thinks and speaks of his ship as a "she," never an "it."

Navymen always go "on board" a ship, or "in" a ship—never "on" a ship. A favorite saying is, "Seamen go down to the seas *in* ships; landlubbers go to sea *on* ships."

Don't make the mistake around sailormen of calling a ship a boat. A tourist aboard a cruise ship such as the *Queen Elizabeth* brings forth only disgust among seamen by saying, "My boat sails at 8 o'clock." What is the difference between ships and boats? It is largely a matter of size, with the smaller craft being recognized as boats. A salty old Chief Petty Officer with many years of seagoing experience once stated it simply to a group of Midshipmen, saying, "A boat is any craft that can be hoisted aboard a ship—and don't you forget it!" There is one exception allowed: submarine sailors call their submarines "boats" despite the fact that by size alone they are classed as ships. Probably this custom dates from the early days when the subs were known as "pigboats" because of their resemblance in shape and color to young porkers, and because of the way they clustered around their "mother" ships when in harbor.

Most people are aware of the use of "port" and "starboard" to mean the left and right sides of a ship when facing forward. Also "fore" and "after" to mean the front and rear of a ship, and "forward and "aft"

The Captain of the U.S.S. *Asheville* (PG-84) watches from the bridge of his ship during underway training.

Opposite: The superstructure is that part of a ship built above the main deck and used for living or working spaces. U.S.S. *Oklahoma City* (CLG-5).

to indicate "toward the front" and "toward the rear." The "bow" is the most forward part of the ship, and the "stern" the after part. The length of a ship is the distance from bow to stern, the width from side to side is called the "beam," and the "draft" is the vertical distance from the waterline to the deepest part of the hull.

Almost everyone knows that aboard ship the floors are called "decks," the ceilings are called "overheads," the walls are known as "bulkheads," and the stairs are known as "ladders." When a sailor goes up a ladder to or above the "main" deck (the uppermost deck which extends from bow to stern), he will say, "I'm going topside"; when going back down into the ship, he says, "I'm going below." These are the equivalent of upstairs and downstairs to people who are not accustomed to living in ships.

In an aircraft carrier the superstructure above the flight deck is called the island. U.S.S. *Oriskany* (CVA-34).

A ship's "superstructure" is that portion of the ship built above the main deck and used for living or working spaces. In an aircraft carrier the superstructure above the "flight" deck (that deck used for aircraft landings and takeoffs) is called the "island." The "bridge" of a ship, located in the superstructure or island, is that location where the ship is "conned" or controlled by the Captain and his officers.

When a ship is "underway" (floating free—not attached to a land structure such as a pier, and not having an anchor on the bottom), she is driven through the water by "screws," as the propellers are called.

The screws are large, pusher-type propellers that operate under water at relatively slow speeds—slow, that is, when compared with the puller-type propellers one sees on some airplanes. The screws push the ship through the water at speeds which are measured in "knots." A knot is a measure of speed—not distance. It is a speed of one nautical mile per hour; a nautical mile is 6,080 feet, slightly longer than a mile on land, because of its derivation by early navigators from geographic measures—i.e., one nautical mile equals one minute of latitude.

The speed of a ship through the water for a given speed of rotation of her screws depends upon a number of factors: her condition of loading (she may be expected to move more slowly when heavily loaded than when empty), the resistance or push exerted on her superstructure and hull by high winds, the state of the sea (high waves may slow her down or may even at times expose her screws, causing loss of propulsion efficiency), and the condition of her bottom (growth of weeds or barnacles slow her down). Nevertheless, each ship has a "rated speed" at which she is expected to travel at each speed of rotation of her screws. This is the speed expected under normal conditions for each hull type, and is usually established by "speed trials" when the ship is new. The expression "rated speed" refers to the maximum speed at which the ship can conduct sustained operations.

Ships are organized into "fleets" and "task forces" for operational control and for best performance of their required operations and tasks. A fleet is the many ships of different types under the operational control of a fleet commander, such as "Commander, First Fleet." A task force is a smaller grouping of certain types of ships organized to accomplish a specific task, or tasks. For example, a "Fast Carrier Task Force" includes the aircraft carriers to conduct air operations against an enemy, the cruisers to provide gun and missile protection against other ships and aircraft, and the escorting destroyers and frigates to provide protection against submarines and aircraft. These are the Navy "teams" which band together ships of different types to accomplish their "tasks" and "missions" as a cohesive unit.

One other nautical term is pertinent. The weight of a ship is known as her "displacement"—the weight of the volume of water the ship displaces or occupies when she floats. When speaking of the weight of his ship, a sailor will say, "She displaces 40,000 tons," or "Her full load displacement is 40,000 tons."

All of these expressions are used by men of the sea when speaking of ships.

SHIP NAMES

Navy ships have names that contain a great deal of information about the ship. There are four parts to a name—for example, consider the U.S.S. *Enterprise* (CVAN–65).

The first part, U.S.S., stands for United States Ship and is a part of the name of every *commissioned* ship in the U.S. Navy—that is, every ship that has been officially commissioned as a member of our Navy.

The second part, *Enterprise*, is the actual name. Names are assigned by rules which will be explained later. Since *Enterprise* is the name which was formerly carried by a number of famous ships in our history, those who are familiar with Navy history and traditions know that it now indicates an aircraft carrier.

The third part of the name, CVAN, tells what type of ship this is. CVA is the Navy designation for the aircraft carriers which carry attack type aircraft, and the N denotes a ship having nuclear propulsion.

Finally, the fourth part of the name, 65, is the "hull number." Hull numbers are normally assigned in sequence for each type of ship; so 65 means that *Enterprise* is the 65th aircraft carrier commissioned in the U.S. Navy. This number is also the number painted on the ship's bow (and the island and flight deck of an aircraft carrier), and so is sometimes called the "bow number" as well.

Thus, by the name U.S.S. *Enterprise* (CVAN–65), we know that this is a commissioned ship of the U.S. Navy, named *Enterprise* (after one or more famous Navy ships of the past), that she is a nuclear-powered attack carrier, and is the 65th carrier on the Navy rolls.

Each ship of the Navy may be identified in similar fashion—by one who knows the meanings of the ship names and designators.

The island of the U.S.S. *Enterprise* (CVAN-65). The hull number on the island can be seen in the shadow.

HOW SHIPS ARE NAMED

Ships of the U.S. Navy are named in accordance with traditional rules and customs.

AIRCRAFT CARRIERS are named after famous ships formerly on the Navy list (U.S.S. *Constellation*) or for important battles of prior years (U.S.S. *Midway*). Recently some carriers have been named after famous Presidents of the United States (U.S.S. *John F. Kennedy*). One (U.S.S. *Forrestal*) was named for the first U.S. Secretary of Defense.

BATTLESHIPS are named for states of the United States (U.S.S. *Missouri*).

CRUISERS are named for United States cities (U.S.S. *Chicago*).

FRIGATES are named for noted U.S. Admirals (U.S.S. *Wainwright*).

DESTROYERS and DESTROYER ESCORTS are named for deceased Navy, Marine Corps, and Coast Guard personnel who served with exceptional bravery or distinction (U.S.S. *Joseph P. Kennedy, Jr.*, U.S.S. *The Sullivans*). They may also be named for Members of Congress (U.S.S. *Hale*), and for Secretaries and Assistant Secretaries of the Navy (U.S.S. *Frank Knox*).

SUBMARINES are named after fish and sea creatures (U.S.S. *Shark*). Fleet Ballistic Missile Submarines are named for famous American statesmen and leaders (U.S.S. *Patrick Henry*).

MINESWEEPERS are named for birds (U.S.S. *Tanager*) or are given names of "logical, fine-sounding words" (U.S.S. *Skill*, U.S.S. *Sturdy*).

OILERS and TANKERS are named for rivers with Indian names (U.S.S. *Guadalupe*).

AMMUNITION SHIPS are named for volcanoes (U.S.S. *Vesuvius*) and words that suggest fire or explosives (U.S.S. *Nitro*).

DESTROYER TENDERS are named for localities and areas of the United States (U.S.S. *Dixie*).

SUBMARINE TENDERS are named for men who did early work in submarine development (U.S.S. *Sperry*) and for characters in mythology (U.S.S. *Apollo*).

STORE SHIPS are named for heavenly bodies (U.S.S. *Sirius*).

HOSPITAL SHIPS are named for words that suggest their mission, such as U.S.S. *Haven*, U.S.S. *Sanctuary*.

A fireman operates the main control panel in the engine room aboard the guided missile frigate, U.S.S. *Wainwright* (DLG-28).

SHIP TYPES AND DESIGNATIONS

Ships of different types are given different letter designations. Although there is no exact meaning in the letters assigned, most of them were developed in a logical manner. For example, auxiliary ships have designators beginning with the letter "A." "AD," the designation for Destroyer Tenders, could be interpreted as "Auxiliary Ship for Destroyers." "DL," the designation for Frigate, probably was derived from "Destroyer Leader," or "Destroyer, Large." Ships with "L" as the first letter in their designations are generally those used in amphibious warfare (Landing Ships). BB denotes Battleships, DD indicates Destroyers, SS identifies Submarines, while the first letter "C" may stand for either Cruiser or Carrier, depending on the other letters used.

The second and third letters in the designations similarly indicate something more about the ship. CVA, for example, designates a Carrier of airplanes (V is the Navy letter designator for heavier-than-air,

Left: Cooks of the U.S.S. *Coral Sea* (CVA-43) standing by one of the two serving lines of the after mess deck.

Opposite: Crew having noon meal aboard the U.S.S. *Ticonderoga* (CVA-14).

fixed-wing aircraft) used for Attack. CVS denotes a carrier of aircraft for anti-submarine Support, and CVT denotes an aircraft carrier used for Training. A number of similar relationships can be noted by examining different ship types and their corresponding designations.

There are a few special letters that are used as part of the designation of all types of ships: "E" before the designator means that the ship is Experimental, "G" after a designator indicates that the ship is equipped with Guided Missiles, and the letter "N" after the designator denotes a ship with Nuclear power.

Although ship *types* are clearly identified by letter designations, the letters do not show which *class* the ship belongs to. The type refers to the basic category of ship, such as Battleship (BB), Submarine (SS), Destroyer (DD), and the like. However, within each *type* of ship there may be a number of different classes. This happens because over a period of years one or more ships of the same type may be built to essentially the same set of plans (same class)—they are similar in length, beam, displacement, and general arrangement —while others of the same type may be built to a different design and thereby become a different class.

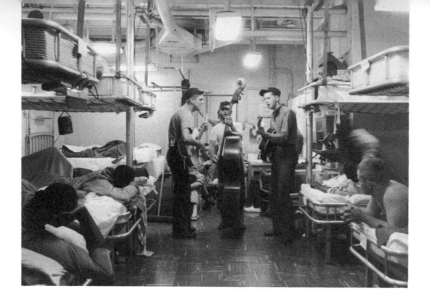

Impromptu entertainment by three sailors aboard the U.S.S. *Iwo Jima* (LPH-2).

Thus a destroyer is given an individual name and also a class name, since she may be one of the *Sherman* (DD-931) class, or the *Sumner* (DD-692) class, or the *Fletcher* (DD-445) class, meaning that it is similar to the other ships of that particular "model" or class. For example, U.S.S. *Mullany* (DD-528) is a *Fletcher* class destroyer.

The classes are named after the first ship of the new design commissioned, and usually the ships in that class have hull numbers in sequence immediately following the first ship of the class. How many ships are in each class depends upon the shipbuilding program in effect while that particular design is considered to be the best available—that is, until some new design or model is approved for building and a new class started.

There are over a hundred different types of ships in the U.S. Navy, each with a different designation. Each type may contain a number of different classes, but the class cannot be determined from the letter designations. Listed below are the most common or most representative types and their assigned letter designations.

DESIGNATION	TYPE OF SHIP	DESIGNATION	TYPE OF SHIP
AD	Destroyer Tender	CVT	Training Aircraft Carrier
AE	Ammunition Ship	DD	Destroyer
AF	Store Ship	DE	Escort Ship
AGMR	Major Communications Relay Ship	DER	Radar Picket Escort Ship
AGS	Surveying Ship	DL	Frigate
AH	Hospital Ship	FDL	Fast Deployment Logistics Ship
AK	Cargo Ship	LCC	Amphibious Command Ship
AO	Oiler	LKA	Amphibious Cargo Ship
AOE	Fast Combat Support Ship	LPA	Amphibious Transport
AP	Transport	LPD	Amphibious Transport, Dock
AR	Repair Ship	LPH	Amphibious Assault Ship
ARS	Salvage Ship	LPSS	Amphibious Transport Submarine
AS	Submarine Tender	LSD	Landing Ship, Dock
ATF	Fleet Ocean Tug	LST	Landing Ship, Tank
ATS	Salvage Tug	MSA	Minesweeper, Auxiliary
AV	Seaplane Tender	MSC	Minesweeper, Coastal
BB	Battleship	MSI	Minesweeper, Inshore
CA	Heavy Cruiser	MSO	Minesweeper, Ocean
CC	Command Ship	PCER	Patrol Rescue Escort
CG	Guided Missile Cruiser	PCF	Patrol Craft, Inshore
CL	Light Cruiser	PG	Patrol Gunboat
CVA	Attack Aircraft Carrier	SS	Submarine
CVS	ASW Support Aircraft Carrier	SSB	Fleet Ballistic Missile Submarine

Part 1 — AIRCRAFT CARRIERS

The Aircraft Carrier is the most important member of the modern Navy team and the backbone of today's powerful task forces. It is the first new type of warship produced in this century; its introduction revolutionized naval warfare.

A carrier is a mobile air base which can operate in international waters on all parts of the globe, and with great speed and power be on the scene and in action rapidly whenever needed. The carrier's mission is to use her aircraft to control the air around and above the operating area, denying to any enemy the advantage of having free access to that area. With squadrons of fighter, bomber, and reconnaissance aircraft aboard, the carrier provides close air support for troops ashore, protection of friendly ships and boats, and reconnaissance information on enemy movements and installations. The reconnaissance aircraft also provide detection and constant surveillance of all submarines and surface ships over a wide area, calling on attack aircraft where necessary to protect our forces. Thus, a carrier task force can apply the precise force required in any situation, and provide strong support whenever trouble arises.

There are three primary types of aircraft carriers: (1) The Attack Aircraft Carrier (CVA) carries the fighters, bombers, and other types of aircraft used to attack an enemy. (2) The Anti-Submarine Support Aircraft Carrier (CVS) carried the aircraft used to seek out and defend against enemy submarines. The CVS usually operates with an Anti-Submarine Task Group (Hunter-Killer Group), and teams up with Destroyers and other surface ships in performing its Anti-Submarine Warfare (ASW) mission. (3) The Training Carriers (CVT) are used to train Navy, Marine Corps, and Air Force pilots in the precision flying necessary to operate successfully at sea and aboard ship.

U.S.S. ENTERPRISE (CVAN-65)
Enterprise is the world's largest warship, and the first nuclear-powered aircraft carrier ever built. She was commissioned in November, 1961, and has since made a number of remarkable records. In 1964, *Enterprise*, with Nuclear Task Force One, circumnavigated the world — cruising over 30,000 miles without taking on fuel or provisions. Theoretically she could cruise eight times around the globe without need to renew her nuclear fuel. She is 1,123 feet in length, with a maximum beam

U.S.S. *Enterprise*

U.S.S. *Kitty Hawk*

(flight deck) of 257 feet and a maximum draft of 37 feet. Her flight deck has an area of about 4½ acres —three football fields could be placed on the flight deck area. Main engines generate up to 360,000 horsepower, which will drive her at speeds of over 30 knots. She has a crew of more than 4,000 officers and men and normally carries about 90 aircraft. Full load displacement is 86,000 tons.

U.S.S. KITTY HAWK (CVA-63)   Commissioned in April, 1961, she is the first of four modern large carriers in the *Kitty Hawk* class. Others in this class are U.S.S. *Constellation* (CVA-64), U.S.S. *America* (CVA-66), and U.S.S. *John F. Kennedy* (CVA-67). These ships are 1,047½ feet long, with a maximum beam of 252 feet and a 37-foot maximum draft. Main engines capable of generating 280,000 horsepower give them a rated speed of 34 knots. Each carries a crew of over 4,000 and has more than 70 aircraft. Full load displacement is 78,000 tons.

U.S.S. FORRESTAL (CVA-59)   Commissioned in October, 1955, *Forrestal* is the only ship in her class, but is similar to the *Saratoga* class, differing in being slightly shorter and with a lesser displacement. In appear-

U.S.S. *Forrestal*

U.S.S. Midway

ance, they are much alike. *Saratoga* class includes U.S.S. *Saratoga* (CVA-60), U.S.S. *Ranger* (CVA-61), and U.S.S. *Independence* (CVA-62). *Forrestal* has a length overall of 1,039 feet, while the other three are 1,046 feet overall. *Forrestal's* full load displacement is 76,000 tons; that of *Saratoga* class ships is 78,700 tons. In other respects they are the same: beam is 252 feet, draft is 37 feet, and all carry more than 70 aircraft and a crew of over 4,000 officers and men. *Forrestal* has slightly less power in her main engines (260,000 horsepower), giving a rated speed of 33 knots. *Saratoga* class ships have main engines of 280,-000 horsepower, and rated speed of 34 knots.

U.S.S. MIDWAY (CVA-41)

First commissioned in 1945, just after World War II, *Midway* is the leader of the first class of "Big Carriers" which the Navy looked toward in the postwar years. Others in the class are U.S.S. *Franklin D. Roosevelt* (CVA-42) and U.S.S. *Coral Sea* (CVA-43). These ships are 979 feet long, with a maximum beam of 222 feet, and a maximum draft of 36 feet. They have a rated speed of 33 knots, carry 70 or more aircraft, and have a crew of over 4,000. Full load displacement is 62,000 tons. *Coral Sea* displaces 63,600 tons. All three ships were completely overhauled and modernized in the middle 1950's, and continue to perform well.

U.S.S. ORISKANY (CVA-34)

Commissioned first in 1950, this ship is the only one of her class, although similar to the older *Hancock* class carriers. Extensively modernized and recommissioned in 1959, *Oriskany*

U.S.S. *Oriskany*

is a capable CVA. Her full load displacement is 42,625 tons, her length is 890 feet, maximum beam is 195 feet, and her main engines turn up 150,000 horsepower, yet her rated speed is 33 knots and she carries a crew of over 4,000 and more than 70 aircraft, holding her own with the larger, more modern carriers.

U.S.S. BENNINGTON (CVS-20)

"Big Ben" is a World War II carrier, first commissioned in August, 1944, modernized in 1955, and converted from a CVA to an Anti-Submarine support carrier in 1959. One of eleven modernized *Essex* class carriers used for ASW, she has a length of 894 feet overall, a maximum beam of 196 feet, and a maximum draft of 31 feet. She has a rated speed of 31 knots, from main engines of 150,000 horsepower. Her crew numbers in excess of 2,300 officers and men, and she carries more than 45 aircraft. Full load displacement is 41,900 tons.

U.S.S. Bennington

U.S.S. *Bennington* and destroyers in formation

Part 2 — BATTLESHIPS AND CRUISERS

Battleships and Cruisers are designed to be able to fight battles at sea against heavy enemy ships, using their large guns and heavy armor plate to best advantage. Unlike the carriers which must rely on their aircraft for their primary protection, the battleships and cruisers protect themselves with their own guns and missiles; they are the "big gun" ships of today's Navy. Their mission is to engage enemy ships with long-range gunfire, to deliver heavy and continuous bombardment against enemy shore installations, and, by means of anti-aircraft guns and missiles, to provide protection to the task force against enemy aircraft. In addition, they frequently serve as flagships and carry both the staff and the communications equipment necessary for the commander to conduct at-sea operations of large task forces.

The designation of "heavy cruiser" (CA) and "light cruiser" (CL) refers only to the armament carried, not to the size or displacement of the ship. CAs carry larger than 6-inch guns, while CLs carry 6-inch and smaller guns. The same is true of the heavy and light guided missile cruisers (CAGs and CLGs), the only difference being that some but not all of their gun turrets have been replaced with missile batteries. Guided missile cruisers (CGs) are pure missile ships, with no main battery guns.

With the advent of modern high-performance aircraft and nuclear weapons, large, costly ships such as battleships were considered by some planners to be vulnerable to air attack. In addition, battleships, employing large crews and having many operating equipments, became costly to operate—particularly in peacetime when their big guns were not immediately required. All U.S. battleships were decommissioned and placed in "mothballs"—a state of preservation from which they can be rapidly returned to active duty if required. They are ready for recommissioning and further service should their large caliber guns be required in any future hostilities.

U.S.S. NEW JERSEY (BB-62)
One of four BBs remaining on the List of Naval Ships (Navy Vessels Register), *New Jersey* is the only one now in commission, having been recommissioned in April, 1968, in order to provide gunfire support to our forces in Vietnam. All four are *Iowa* class battleships; the three not now in commission are U.S.S. *Iowa* (BB-61), U.S.S. *Missouri* (BB-63), and U.S.S. *Wisconsin* (BB-64).

62

U.S.S. New Jersey

U.S.S. *Long Beach*

All are 887 feet in length, with a beam of 108 feet and a draft of 38 feet maximum. Displacement is 59,300 tons, and the full wartime crew is 2,700 officers and men. Their main engines generate 212,000 horsepower, driving the ships with a rated speed of 31 knots. *New Jersey*, with her nine 16-inch guns, each capable of hurling 2,700-pound projectiles more than 20 miles with pinpoint precision, is able to give strong gunfire support to our forces operating against an enemy in coastal regions. Her steel armor plate (16 inches thick on turrets and conning tower, 12 inches thick along her sides, and 5 inches thick on her armor deck) provides protection to vital spaces against all but the largest bombs, missiles, and projectiles.

U.S.S. LONG BEACH (CGN-9)

The Navy's first nuclear-powered surface ship, the guided missile cruiser *Long Beach*, was commissioned in September, 1961. Her main battery consists of Surface-to-Air Missiles (SAMs)—two Terrier twin launchers forward, and a single Talos twin launcher aft. Twin nuclear reactors generate steam to drive *Long Beach* at speeds in excess of 30 knots, and during Operation Sea Orbit, as a member of Nuclear Task Force One, she traveled around the world without taking on fuel or provisions. Her length overall is 721 feet, her beam is 73 feet, and her maximum draft is 26 feet. Full load displacement is 16,250 tons. Her large, boxlike superstructure is an oddity among cruisers. It, like the island of *Enterprise*, carries large radar antennas on each of the flat faces of the structure.

U.S.S. CHICAGO (CG-11)

Another missile cruiser, but one without the nuclear power of the *Long Beach*, *Chicago* has Talos guided missiles fore and aft, with Tartar missiles amidships. She is a member of the *Albany* class, with two sister-ships in the class: U.S.S. *Albany* (CG-10) and U.S.S. *Columbus* (CG-12). All were converted from heavy cruisers into their present configuration as guided missile cruisers. An unusual

U.S.S. *Oklahoma City*

feature is their use of tall "MACKS" (combined masts and stacks) to support radar antennas as well as to exhaust the fireroom gases as do conventional stacks. Their length is 674 feet, beam 71 feet, and maximum draft 27 feet. Displacing 17,800 tons, and with main engines which develop 120,000 horsepower, these ships have a rated speed of 33 knots. They carry crews of 1,700 officers and men.

U.S.S. OKLAHOMA CITY (CLG-5)   A converted light cruiser (CL), this is one of six such conversions which retain the original 6-inch guns forward, but replace the after gun batteries with Surface-to-Air Missiles. CLGs numbers 3 through 8 displace 14,400 tons, full load, and are 610 feet long, with a beam of 66 feet and a draft of 25 feet. Each carries a crew of 1,200 officers and men, and has a rated speed of 32 knots.

U.S.S. CANBERRA (CA-70)   (formerly CAG-2) The second of two heavy cruisers forming the *Boston* (CA-69) class, *Canberra* retains her 8-inch guns in the two forward turrets, and mounts two twin Terrier batteries aft as secondary batteries. Both ships of the class displace 17,000 tons full load, and carry crews of more than 1,700 officers and men. Their designation was changed to CAG-1 and CAG-2, but has since

U.S.S. *Newport News*

148

reverted to the CA designation. With main engines of 120,000 horsepower, they are capable of 33 knots rated speed. Their length is 673 feet, beam is 71 feet, and maximum draft is 29 feet. *Canberra* was the Navy's first combatant ship equipped with satellite communications equipment; the antenna may be seen mounted atop the foremast. Installed in 1965, this equipment permitted *Canberra* to communicate reliably over thousands of miles by means of the SYNCOM relay satellite.

U.S.S. NEWPORT NEWS (CA-148)
Very few "all-gun" cruisers remain in commission now that guided missiles have become so important in modern warfare. For pinpoint accuracy in bombardment of enemy fortifications ashore, however, there is no substitute for fast, mobile naval gunfire. *Newport News*, with her nine 8-inch guns, is typical of the heavy cruisers—many of which are today in "mothballs," but could be recommissioned on short notice if their gunfire support were needed. *Newport News* is in the *Salem* class, along with U.S.S. *Des Moines* (CA-134) and U.S.S. *Salem* (CA-139). All are World War II designs, proved by years of wartime service to be fine ships. *Newport News* and her sister-ships have a full load displacement of 21,500 tons, length of 716½ feet, beam of 76½ feet, and maximum draft of 26 feet. Their main engines generate 120,000 horsepower, driving the ships at a rated speed of 33 knots. Each carries a crew of 1,860 officers and men.

Part 3 — FRIGATES AND DESTROYERS

The destroyer types are the most versatile of our Navy's warships. Their duties range from bombardment of enemy shore installations to blockading shipping and providing vital defense against enemy submarines and aircraft. Essentially lightly constructed, fast, highly maneuverable ships, the "tin cans" (so called because of their thin steel, unarmored hulls) depend upon speed and firepower rather than on armor for protection.

Frigates are a post-World War II addition to the destroyer Navy. They are Destroyer Leaders, or Destroyer Large (DL), type ships—having the required space and additional equipment needed to accommodate the commander of destroyer forces at sea, as well as the stability and heavy-weather resistance needed for special missions.

The missions of the Frigate and Destroyer are many. They provide gunfire support to forces ashore, and their speed and maneuverability make them excellent patrol and intercept ships to prevent enemy ships from entering protected zones. (The name "destroyer" evolved from their first use, that of "torpedo boat destroyer.") They also are excellent air defense ships; most of their guns are dual-purpose—that is, they can be used for either surface targets or air targets. One important mission is protection against submarines. All are equipped with SONAR (SOund Navigation And Ranging) equipment for detecting and tracking submerged submarines, and a number of weapons for attacking them. Their speed and maneuverability also make them excellent ships for detecting, tracking, and destroying enemy submarines. Finally, their mission includes the use of their torpedoes against enemy ships if such attacks become possible.

With such a versatile ship, the Navy needs are for large numbers both in peacetime and wartime. The U.S. Navy usually has several hundred in commission, made up of many different classes of destroyers and frigates. The newer classes tend to be larger in order that they may carry the modern missiles and other equipment needed for proper performance of the ship's mission.

The frigates (DLG) have missile batteries, and a number of destroyers (DDG) are either being built with guided missile batteries, or older destroyers (DD) are being converted to carry missiles in addition to their 5-inch and 3-inch guns. Some of the newest frigates are nuclear-powered (DLGN), as well as being equipped with guided missile batteries. All are designed to provide the speed, endurance, and seakeeping qualities necessary to provide protection against air, surface, and sub-surface threats.

U.S.S. BAINBRIDGE (DLGN-25)

The first nuclear-powered frigate, *Bainbridge* was also the first of the very large destroyer-type ships—approaching cruiser size. She was commissioned in October of 1962, and is the only ship of her class. Displacing 8,700 tons, full load, with a 564-foot length, a 58-foot beam, and a 24½-foot maximum draft, she uses two nuclear reactors to generate more than 60,000 horsepower and drive her at greater than 30-knot speeds. A "double ender" (missile launchers both fore and aft), her armament consists of four 3-inch guns, two twin Terrier missile launchers, and an ASROC (Anti-Submarine Rocket) launcher. Her crew numbers 400 officers and men. She participated in the circumnavigation of the globe in 1964 by Nuclear Task Force One, cruising 30,216 nautical miles without taking on fuel or provisions.

U.S.S. *Bainbridge*

U.S.S. *Truxtun*

U.S.S. TRUXTUN (DLGN-35)
The second nuclear frigate, an even larger model than the *Bainbridge*, was commissioned in 1966. Her length of 565 feet, beam of 58 feet, and maximum draft of 30 feet give her a displacement of 9,050 tons, full load. Her main engines generate above 60,000 horsepower, for a rated speed exceeding 30 knots. She carries one twin Terrier launcher, one 5-inch gun, and DASH (Drone Anti-

Submarine Helicopter) for conducting ASW operations with a "Drone" (remote-controlled, unmanned) helicopter.

U.S.S. BELKNAP (DLG-26)   The first of a new class of nine DLGs, *Belknap* was commissioned in November of 1964. Smaller than the DLGNs, these ships carry the same armament as the *Truxtun*, and operate with the same size crew (400), with a rated speed of 34 knots. Their length is 547 feet, beam 55 feet, and maximum draft 29 feet. Full load displacement is 7,900 tons.

U.S.S. *Belknap*

U.S.S. Farragut

U.S.S. FARRAGUT (DLG-6)   *Farragut* is the lead ship of ten DLGs of a class commissioned between 1959 and 1961. DLG 6 through 15 are "single enders" (guided missiles either forward or aft—not both) with a 5-inch gun forward and a twin Terrier missile launcher aft. Full load displacement is 5,350 tons. Length is 512½ feet, beam is 52½ feet, and maximum draft is 25 feet. With 4 boilers generating 85,000 horsepower, their rated speed is 34 knots.

U.S.S. CHARLES F. ADAMS (DDG-2)   The first of 23 general-purpose Anti-Air Warfare/Anti-Submarine Warfare (AAW/ASW) destroyers, *Adams* was commissioned in September, 1960. Although the basic hull design is the same for all of the *Adams* class (DDG 2 through 24), there are differences in armament and detection equipment carried. Their major characteristics are: length, 432 feet; beam, 47 feet; maximum draft, 20 feet; and displacement, 4,500 tons. Their 80,000-horsepower engines drive them at a rated speed of 35 knots. Each crew numbers 354 officers and men. Basic armament for the class is two single-mount 5-inch guns, one forward and one aft, an ASROC installation amidships, and a twin Tartar guided missile launcher aft.

U.S.S. Charles F. Adams

U.S.S. Somers

U.S.S. SOMERS (DDG-34)   Originally a *Hull* class Destroyer (DD-947), *Somers* was converted to a DDG in 1964 after being originally commissioned in 1959. One of four such conversions (DDG 31 through 34), she retains the single mount 5-inch gun forward, but replaces the two gun mounts aft with DASH facilities and a Tartar missile launcher. The basic characteristics of the DDG-31 type, like the *Forrest Sherman/Hull* class from which converted, are: length, 418 feet; beam, 45 feet; draft, 20 feet; and displacement approximately 4,000 tons. Their engines generate 70,000 horsepower for a rated speed of 33 knots.

U.S.S. SARSFIELD (DD-837)   The largest and probably most dependable class of destroyers ever built by the Navy is the *Sumner* (692) class, and its later "long hull" version, the *Gearing* (710) class. This World War II design produced over 200 ships, many of which are still in active service. All have been extensively

U.S.S. *Sarsfield*

U.S.S. Cogswell

modified through a number of FRAM (Fleet Rehabilitation and Modernization Program) overhauls, and in the process have been classified into several new classes; however, *Sarsfield* is representative of most of the general-purpose destroyers. She has the basic "long hull" design, 3,500-ton displacement, 390-foot length overall, 41-foot beam, and 21-foot maximum draft. Her four boilers generate 60,000 horsepower for a rated speed of 34 knots. Her crew is 350 officers and men. Armament among members of the class varies widely; that of *Sarsfield* is representative: four 5-inch dual-purpose guns in two twin mounts, one forward and one aft. An ASROC launcher amidships and a DASH installation aft complete her ASW (Anti-Submarine Warfare) weapons.

U.S.S. COGSWELL (DD-651)
A few of the pre-World War II *Fletcher* class (DD-445) 2,100-ton destroyers are still on active duty, having served well for almost 30 years. The workhorse of the destroyer force during World War II, this design has proved to be extremely able in all situations. A number of the *Fletchers* have been sold or loaned to friendly nations; others have been extensively modified for further service in the U.S. Navy. *Cogswell*, after being decommissioned in the late '40s, was recommissioned in 1950 to take part in the Korean War, and has been in service since that time. One of her original 5-inch guns has been replaced with a 3-inch twin mount, but the remaining four 5-inchers are as first installed, in single mounts, two forward and two aft. Her length is 376 feet, beam is 40 feet, and draft is 18 feet; driven by main engines of 60,000 horsepower, she attains a rated speed of 35 knots. Her crew numbers 300 officers and men.

Part 4 — SUBMARINES

Submarines have long played an important part in warfare at sea. From their earliest uses for patrol and scouting, planting "mines" and explosive charges, and attacking enemy shipping, they have relied primarily upon their ability to stay hidden beneath the surface—and that is still one of their most important assets.

The addition of nuclear power has greatly increased the importance of submarines, for now they are true submersibles which can stay under the ocean for weeks or months and can cruise at great speeds while submerged. Both of these, long submergence and great submerged speed, are capabilities that were not possible when submarines relied upon diesel engines, requiring air and fuel, and electric storage batteries, requiring frequent recharging. Since they can be designed for almost unlimited submerged operations, nuclear-powered boats can have hull forms especially adapted to higher submerged speeds than are possible on the surface.

The use of atomic fuel gives a submarine almost unlimited cruising range at top speed without the need for frequent refueling. Some strategists believe that future navies may be largely submarine-type ships, retaining their original missions, but relying on staying submerged to protect them from enemy missiles.

Today's Navy submarines have a number of missions. They perform tactical functions of patrol, reconnaissance, attacking enemy shipping, and detecting and attacking enemy submarines. They are also frequently used as radar picket stations in locations near enemy coastlines, and as rescue stations for downed aircraft crews just off enemy coasts.

In addition, the newest type of submarines, the Fleet Ballistic Missile (FBM) submarines, perform strategic functions. Carrying as many as 16 Polaris missiles which have a range of more than 1,500 miles, these submarines can remain submerged and hidden from detection in waters well within range of the enemy's important targets. The fact that the U.S. Navy has this capability is a strong deterrent against any potential enemy who may otherwise attempt to start a surprise war, hoping to knock out all U.S. offensive weapons on the first attack. Thus, the hidden Polaris submarines, armed with powerful missiles

U.S.S. James Madison

U.S.S. Robert E. Lee

with nuclear warheads, are used in the strategic warfare of prevention of future wars.

With 41 Polaris FBM submarines in commission, an average of 22 are kept on station at all times, ready to retaliate for any enemy attack against the United States. They deploy submerged for sixty-day patrols with pre-targeted missiles capable of being fired from beneath the surface. Each boat has two complete crews, one called the Blue crew and one called the Gold crew. The crews, each having 130 officers and men, alternate on patrols, thus relieving somewhat the monotony of two months of submerged operations by permitting a time ashore for leaves, schooling, and training while the alternate crew is on patrol.

U.S.S. JAMES MADISON (SSBN-627)

One of the 31 *Lafayette* (616) class FBM submarines, *Madison* has been modified to allow carrying the improved A-3 Polaris missile, which has a range of 2,500 nautical miles. These are very large submarines, displacing 8,250 tons submerged and 7,250 tons when on the surface. They are able to travel at speeds greater than 20 knots submerged and 15 knots on the surface. Their length is 425 feet, maximum beam (as it is for all FBM boats) is 33 feet, and their draft when surfaced is 28 feet.

U.S.S. ROBERT E. LEE (SSBN-601)

One of the earlier FBM boats, *Lee* is a member of the *George Washington* (598) class, a class of five boats which were commissioned in 1959 through 1961. This class is the smallest of the FBMs, displacing 6,700 tons submerged, and only 382 feet long. Their speed, like all of the FBMs, is rated in excess of 15 knots surfaced and 20 knots submerged. Close examination of photographs of surfaced FBMs reveals the 16 Polaris missile hatches in the enlarged hull section just aft of the conning tower. A later class, the *Ethan Allen* (608) class, is between the 598 class and the 616 class in size. The *Ethan Allen* class boats are five in number; they displace 6,900 tons submerged, and are 410 feet long. The *George Washington* (SSBN-598) scored a historic first when she launched the first operational Polaris A-1 missile from a submerged position off Cape Canaveral on July 27, 1960.

U.S.S. Nautilus

U.S.S. NAUTILUS (SSN-571)

The first atomic-powered ship in the world, *Nautilus* was commissioned in 1954. On January 17, 1955, she electrified the world with her message, "Underway on nuclear power." She proved the feasibility of using nuclear fuel to power ships and opened a new era in naval mobility. Since that time she has achieved a number of important goals, cruising to the North Pole (under the ice) and setting speed and endurance records with just about every cruise. *Nautilus* is classified as an attack submarine, and carries six bow torpedo tubes for launching her weapons. She has a surface speed of 20 knots and a submerged speed of 23 knots; her main engines are estimated to be capable of generating 13,000 horsepower. Displacing 4,091 tons, her 320-foot hull has a beam of 28 feet and a surfaced draft of 22 feet. Her crew numbers 109 officers and men.

U.S.S. TRITON (SSN-586) *Triton,* at the time of commissioning in 1959, was the largest and heaviest submarine in the U.S. Navy. Originally designed to be a radar picket submarine, she needed the size for carrying the complex electronic equipment and the crew to man the radars. She displaces 7,781 tons submerged, and 5,948 tons when on the surface. Her length of 447½ feet, beam of 37 feet, and draft of 24

U.S.S. *Triton*

U.S.S. Wahoo

feet still form the largest submarine hull in the Navy. Her two reactors drive through the water at speeds of 30 knots on the surface and 20 knots submerged; as a radar picket she was designed to operate much of the time on the surface, where she needed high speeds to elude potential enemies.

In 1960, during her shakedown cruise, *Triton* circumnavigated the earth submerged—the first submarine to do so. The total distance traveled was 35,979 nautical miles, and the time required to make the complete trip was approximately 84 days.

U.S.S. WAHOO (SS-565)

Wahoo is an older type of attack submarine, powered by conventional (diesel-electric) main engines which generate 4,000 horsepower and drive her at 20 knots surfaced and 17 knots submerged. Originally commissioned in 1952, she carries a crew of 83.

58

U.S.S. IREX (SS-482)   An old boat of the *Tench* class, *Irex* was built during World War II. Displacing 2,400 tons, 312 feet long, with diesel-electric drive of 4,600 horsepower, she has rated speeds of 20 knots surfaced and 10 knots submerged. She is classed as a Fleet snorkel boat; the snorkel breathing device allows the submarine to operate diesels and cruise or charge batteries while at periscope depth.

U.S.S. *Irex*

Part 5 —AMPHIBIOUS WARFARE SHIPS

The U.S. Navy developed the techniques of modern amphibious warfare in World War II, and has been improving upon them in the years since. To take and hold territory requires that our troops be put on enemy-held shores, equipped to overcome enemy troops and to sustain operations for an indefinite period. The role of the Navy is to transport our troops and their equipment from their bases to the enemy shores, and to land them safely and efficiently. To do so requires a number of different types of ships— each with its own part to play as a member of the Navy amphibious warfare team.

New ships, with greater carrying capacity and greater speed, have been developed for modern amphibious warfare. The advent of the helicopter has played an important part in landing troops ashore. Helicopters allow rapid transport of the first wave of soldiers or Marines from the large ships which brought them to the battle area. Landing behind the enemy lines, they can quickly establish a beachhead for the waves of assault boats carrying heavy support equipment and other troops. Such new tactics require new types of ships; these have been developed to enhance our Navy's amphibious warfare capabilities.

The primary mission of the amphibious forces is to land troops on enemy-controlled territory. Using command ships (LCC) to direct and control an assault landing, personnel transport ships (LPA) and cargo ships (LKA) to carry troops and equipment, tank landing ships (LST) to transport the heavy tanks and trucks to the beach, and a variety of support ships of different types, the Navy has become adept at carrying out this mission. The amphibious ships are well supported by gunfire from escorting cruisers and destroyers, bombing and strafing by aircraft from nearby carriers, and are provided air defense and defense against submarines by units of supporting task forces.

U.S.S. IWO JIMA (LPH-2)   The LPH is a relatively new type of amphibious ship, one designed to carry helicopters and troops for making airborne assaults on or behind beachheads. *Iwo Jima* is the lead ship of a seven-ship class of LPH. Commissioned in 1961, she normally carries about 2,000 troops and from 20 to 30 assault helicopters, and can proceed to assault areas at speeds as high as her rated top of 20

U.S.S. *Iwo Jima*

U.S.S. *Estes*

knots. The *Iwo Jima* class ships displace 18,000 tons, and are 592 feet long, with a 105-foot beam, and 26-foot draft. They are known as Amphibious Assault Ships.

U.S.S. ESTES (LCC-12)   *Estes* is one of a number of Amphibious Command Ships, previously known as Amphibious Force Flagships (AGC). They are used as the command headquarters for amphibious operations. Located aboard these ships are the commanders of both the ship forces and the landing forces involved in the amphibious assaults. These Navy Admirals and Army and Marine Corps Generals and their staffs plan, direct, and control the landing operations from the command ships. *Estes* was built to Navy contract from a basic Maritime Commission design (C2) in 1943. Her full load displacement is 14,400 tons, and her length is 459 feet. She has a rated speed of 16 knots.

U.S.S. BEXAR (LPA-237)   The primary troop carrier is the LPA, Attack Transport, whose previous letter designation was APA. *Bexar* is typical of many such ships, a majority of which are now in the reserve fleet (mothballs) until needed. These are mostly converted World War II merchant-type ships originally

KA 104

U.S.S. *Seminole*

called (VC2) "Victory Ships," which were adapted to Navy needs. They displace about 10,000 tons, are 455 feet long, and are rated at maximum speeds of 18 knots. Each can carry 2,500 tons of cargo and 2,500 troops. All such ships are equipped with many small landing craft (assault boats) which are used to transport the troops and their equipment ashore.

U.S.S. SEMINOLE (LKA-104)

The LKA type was previously known as AKA; they are Attack Cargo Ships which carry the necessary "assault loaded combat cargo" for amphibious landings. The most vital cargo (food, guns, ammunition, clothing, medical supplies, etc.) is stowed near the top of the holds so as to be sent to the beachhead with the first assault waves, followed by the cargo necessary to sustain an operation after the beachhead is secured. *Seminole* is a converted merchant cargo type of ship (C2), first commissioned in the Navy in 1945. She displaces 10,000 tons, is 459 feet long, and has a rated top speed of 17 knots. She can carry 2,000 tons of assault loaded cargo. She also carries as many as 24 landing craft (assault boats) to offload the cargo and ferry it in to the beaches when needed. Her many booms on the decks are for offloading the boats and then lifting the heavy cargo from deep in the holds of the ship into the boats.

U.S.S. PERCH (LPSS-313)

A somewhat different type of troop transport, *Perch* is a submarine equipped for carrying a small number of troops for very special, covert landings in enemy territory. Approaching

U.S.S. *Perch*

U.S.S. Monticello

enemy territory submerged, this type of Amphibious Transport Submarine may surface just off enemy coasts under cover of darkness and disembark her troops in rubber boats for the actual landing. The LPSS may then submerge and wait to pick up her landing party at an appointed spot and time after the mission is completed. *Perch* is an old type of diesel-electric submarine which is 312 feet long and displaces about 2,400 tons submerged. She has rated speeds of 20 knots on the surface and 10 knots submerged.

U.S.S. MONTICELLO (LSD-35)   The Dock Landing Ship is built around a drydocklike well which may be flooded or drained dry as desired. Thus, the ship may be used as a drydock for small ships and boats—or, as more often happens, she may carry fully loaded landing craft in the dry well. When in the landing area, she floods the dock and opens the stern gate, allowing the craft to become waterborne and depart rapidly for the beach. *Monticello,* commissioned in 1958, is one of the eight-ship *Thomaston* class—510 feet long, 11,270 tons full load displacement, and with a rated speed of 21 knots. She carries a crew of about 300 and has cranes capable of lifting 50 tons—important assets to her drydock work and assault craft loading. She may carry as many as 21 assault boats.

U.S.S. OGDEN (LPD-5)   Still another new member of the Landing Force Team, the Amphibious Transport, Dock, combines the functions of an Amphibious Transport (LPA), Dock Landing Ship (LSD), and

U.S.S. Ogden

U.S.S. Wood County

an Amphibious Assault Ship (LPH). *Ogden* is the second of fifteen ships which displace 17,150 tons when fully loaded, are 581 feet long, and are capable of speeds of 21 knots, allowing them to make fast approaches to the assault area. She, like the LSD, can launch pre-loaded landing craft from the well deck of her stern. The platform above the well deck is the landing pad for helicopters which may make vertical assaults, in the style of the LPH. *Ogden* may carry over a thousand troops and their equipment for a landing.

U.S.S. WOOD COUNTY (LST-1178)

The Tank Landing Ships are the most numerous of the larger amphibious vessels. Originally developed in World War II, the LST types revolutionized amphibious warfare by their ability to run up on the beach, drop their ramps on dry land, and offload great quantities of tanks, trucks, and equipment of all kinds. The main load is pre-packed trucks with their cargo for combat in place when they are driven on the ships. Heavy tanks and armored vehicles are also carried. *Wood County* was commissioned in 1959. She is one of seven ships of the LST 1171 class, 445 feet long, 7,100 tons displacement, and with diesel engines capable of driving her at a rated speed of 17 knots. Her maximum displacement is 18 feet, but this is usually the draft aft where the screws are located. By shifting ballast, the forward draft may be decreased to only three or four feet, thus making possible a "dry ramp" landing when the bow is beached. The bow doors are then opened and the ramp is lowered into place for the vehicles to drive off.

Part 6 — ESCORT, PATROL, AND MINE WARFARE SHIPS

In wartime the Navy needs many maneuverable, hard-working ships to perform the functions of escorting and patrolling. It must be prepared to furnish escorts to large numbers of merchant vessels without the ability to defend themselves—they depend upon their Navy escorts for protection against enemy surface ships, submarines, and aircraft. During World War II many merchant convoys were shepherded safely through submarine-infested waters by the nimble, fast escort ships of the Navy—many of which were converted to escort types from other ship designs.

Similar fast, maneuverable ships are used for patrolling and protecting coasts and harbors in friendly territory, or for blockading enemy areas to prevent entry from the sea. In Vietnam, Navy patrols were extended to the many rivers and inlets of that country, and the patrol vessels of importance for those operations were the speedy, heavily armed Patrol Gunboats (PG) and the Inshore Patrol Craft (PCF), better known as "Swift Boats." These types were especially developed and equipped for riverine patrol duty.

Mine warfare ships have characteristics similar to those of escort and patrol vessels. In addition, they have been designed to detect, dislodge, and destroy mines which have been placed in waters where our ships must operate. When not used for mine hunting, the minesweepers may also be used for patrol and escort duties.

The primary mission of all of these versatile ships is one of protection of our larger ships and forces. They are designed for and adapted to the protective role—protection of our ships from enemy sea forces, and protection of our troops ashore from infiltration by enemy troops from the sea and river approaches. The protection against mines is a valuable function—especially for those ships engaged in amphibious operations or other such actions which bring them into shallow waters where mines may have been planted.

The Escort Ships (DE—originally called Destroyer Escorts) are a departure from the rule that most of the escorts are small and light. Modern DE types are becoming large and complex; they resemble the DD types of prior years. In appearance they look like Destroyers but generally are less heavily armed, specializing in the weapons used for ASW (Anti-Submarine Warfare) and AAW (Anti-Aircraft Warfare). They carry the most modern SONAR (SOund Navigation And Ranging) equipment for the location and track-

U.S.S. *Knox*

ing of submerged submarines, and modern weapons such as ASROC (Anti-Submarine ROCket) and DASH (Drone Anti-Submarine Helicopter) for attacking and destroying enemy subs.

U.S.S. KNOX (DE-1052)
The most modern and largest of the DE types, *Knox* is lead ship of a class of 26. Displacing 4,100 tons, full load, with a length of 438 feet, these ships are the equivalent of modern destroyers in all respects except speed and firepower. Their two boilers generate about 35,000 horsepower, giving a rated speed of about 25 knots. The ships of this class have a bow-mounted SONAR projecting beneath the bow.

U.S.S. Davidson

U.S.S. DAVIDSON (DE-1045)   Commissioned in 1965, *Davidson* is one of the 10-ship *Garcia* class of modern, large escorts. Larger than older DE types, but not so large as the *Knox* class, these ships are 414½ feet long and displace 3,400 tons. Their rated 25-knot speed allows them to escort high-speed convoys and task forces, as well as equipping them well for the speed necessary to track fast-moving submarines. Their armament consists of two 5-inch guns, ASROC, and DASH; their SONAR assists in the detection and tracking of enemy subs.

U.S.S. BROOKE (DEG-1)   Lead ship of a class of six guided missile escorts, *Brooke* was commissioned in 1965. Her size and design are similar to that of the *Garcia* class of DE; however, addition of a guided missile battery strengthens her role of AAW escort. She carries a Tartar missile battery in lieu of the after 5-inch gun of the *Garcia* class, and retains the forward 5-incher. She also retains the ASROC and DASH

U.S.S. Brooke

U.S.S. *Evans*

installations, giving her a strong ASW capability. *Brooke* class ships, like *Garcia* and *Knox* classes, carry crews of approximately 200 officers and men. All have rated speeds of about 25 knots.

U.S.S. EVANS (DE-1023)

Evans is the lead ship of a class of eight, and was commissioned in 1957. This class is very much like another, earlier *Dealey* (DE-1006) class. Both are more akin to the older escort ships than to the more modern, but larger, DE classes. *Evans* and *Dealey* classes displace about 1,900 tons, are 314½ feet long, and have maximum drafts of 18 feet. Both classes carry four 3-inch guns and a variety of ASW weapons. They are manned by crews of 170 officers and men.

U.S.S. LEADER (MSO-490)

There are 61 non-magnetic Ocean Minesweepers (MSO) in the *Agile* (MSO-421) class. *Leader* is one of the 61 in the U.S. Navy; a number of additional ships of the same design have been sold to other friendly nations. These ships are 172 feet long, have crews of 72 officers and men, and

490

U.S.S. *Leader*

U.S.S. *Parrot*

displace 760 tons. Their two diesels give them a rated speed of 15 knots. The non-magnetic ships have plywood hulls, diesel engines built with special non-magnetic stainless steel alloys, and other metal fittings made of aluminum, or brass—all to make the ship as resistant as possible to the magnetic influence mines which they may be called upon to sweep. Each minesweeper has long "tails" which are unrolled and towed astern to destroy magnetic mines. The "tails" are heavy electric cables which, connected to gas-turbine-driven electric generators, put large electric currents in the water astern of the ship, creating magnetic fields well away from the ship. These fields set off the magnetic mines and destroy them when they are safely astern and away from the ship. The reason for keeping the ships as non-magnetic as possible is to avoid setting off the mines prematurely. The MSO ships are also equipped to sweep (dislodge or detonate) mines of the acoustic and contact type.

U.S.S. PARROT (MSC-197)

A Coastal Minesweeper, *Parrot* is a member of the 20-ship *Bluebird* (MSC-121) class. These ships have non-magnetic properties like the *Agile* class, and for the same reasons—their methods of sweeping are similar and they require the protection from magnetic influence mines. *Parrot* displaces 370 tons and is 144 feet long. Manned by a crew of 40, her twin diesel engines are capable of driving her at speeds of 14 knots.

U.S.S. CAPE (MSI-2)

Still smaller than the coastal sweepers are the Inshore Minesweepers (MSI). *Cape* is the second ship of the *Cove* (MSI-1) class, the members of which displace 248 tons, are 112 feet long, and have a 9-foot maximum draft. They are manned by crews of 20; their rated top speed is 12 knots. These ships are designed for very close inshore sweeping—shallow bays, rivers, possible approaches for amphibious landings, and the like, are their special fields of operations.

U.S.S. *Cape*

U.S.S. MARATHON (PG-89)   The Patrol Gunboat (PG) class has come into prominence in the Vietnam War, where its powerful firepower and close-in support of shore forces, as well as its speed and maneuverability, are perfect for the type of operations conducted there. *Marathon* was commissioned in 1968, the sixth of the seven-ship *Asheville* (PG-84) class. All have aluminum hulls and fiberglass superstructures. They are 165 feet long and carry a 3-inch gun forward—the largest gun ever mounted on a ship of that size. They also carry 40-millimeter cannon and 50-caliber machine guns. The mission of the PG is to blockade coastal shipping and defend amphibious forces; since the forward 3-inch gun can accurately place fifty 13-pound projectiles a minute in a target area, their firepower is respected by enemies and admired by friendly forces. Main engine of each PG is a 14,000 horsepower J79 gas turbine, similar to those found in high-performance jet aircraft. *Marathon* can go from a standing start to 40 knots in less than a minute. Twin diesels provide power for low-speed, high-endurance cruising.

U.S.S. Marathon

U.S.S. *Tucumcari*

U.S.S. TUCUMCARI (PGH-2)   The second of the *High Point* class of Hydrofoil Gunboats, *Tucumcari* displaces about 57 tons, is about 80 feet long, and is designed to "fly" on her hydrofoils at speeds up to 50 knots. Such high speeds are especially beneficial when the ships are engaged in chase or rescue operations. Hydrofoil ships will normally cruise with their foils retracted. When high speeds are required, they can be expected to lower their foils in the water and increase their speed. Gradually the foils will exert force against the water and provide lift, raising the hull higher, decreasing the drag, and allowing for further increases in speed. As speed increases, the lift increases, until the entire hull may be clear of the water, and the ship "flies" on her foils alone. Instead of screws, *Tucumcari* uses a water-jet propulsion system.

Part 7 — AUXILIARY SHIPS

It has been said that the Navy could start a war without its Auxiliary Ships, but it couldn't keep up the fight for very long. These are the ships that replenish the stores, fuel, food, and ammunition that are used up by the combatant ships during their operations. They may be likened to "the man behind the man behind the gun," although they are frequently so near to the actual fighting that they, too, are a part of it.

There are as many types of auxiliary ships as there are jobs to be done. The tenders carry repair parts and have workshops for all types of repairs. They are "mother ships" for the ships assigned to their care, providing all of the essentials for forward area support. Destroyer Tenders (AD), Submarine Tenders (AS), and Seaplane Tenders (AV) are important auxiliary types; they follow the Fleet and provide the "can do" answer of skilled craftsmen. Repair ships (AR) are similar to tenders, but their work is not limited to any particular types of ships.

Supply ships of all types are part of the auxiliary fleet. Cargo ships (AK), Ammunition ships (AE), Oilers (AO), and Stores ships (AF) carry the food, fuel, and ammunition needed by the ships being supported. As soon as one of the supply ships issues all of its material, it returns to base to take on another load; meanwhile, its place in the supply force has been taken by another with a full load of its vital cargo.

There are many other types of auxiliaries—rescue ships, hospital ships, salvage ships, research ships, tugs—as many types as are needed to keep a fighting fleet in fighting trim.

U.S.S. BRYCE CANYON (AD-36)
One of nine ships built from modified C3 merchant types during World War II, *Bryce Canyon* carries a crew of skilled craftsmen to man the ship and her shops. These Destroyer Tenders serve as floating service stations for the many Destroyers under their care. They are large ships—displacing 16,635 tons, and having an overall length of 492 feet. Their main engines generate 8,500 horsepower, enough to drive the ships at a rated speed of 18.4 knots.

U.S.S. HOLLAND (AS-32)
The Submarine Tenders are similar to the ADs except for their special shops and skills devoted to the needs of submarines and their crews. *Holland* is of the recently built *Hunley* class

U.S.S. *Bryce Canyon*

U.S.S. *Holland*

U.S.S. Currituck

(AS-31), and was commissioned in 1963. These are FBM Submarine Tenders, with the handling and storage equipment as well as the workshops and trained men for servicing the Polaris missiles. These tenders displace 18,300 tons and are 599 feet long. Their main engines are diesels, capable of generating 15,000 horsepower to drive the ships at rated speeds of 18 knots.

U.S.S. CURRITUCK (AV-7)

The lead ship of her three-ship class, this Seaplane Tender was built in the early 1940's to service the seaplanes used for patrol of waters far from established bases. She is 540 feet long, and displaces 15,000 tons. Her steam turbine main engines drive her at a rated speed of 19 knots. She has the large crane which is characteristic of the seaplane tenders. The crane is used to lift the large, heavy planes aboard the tender after they have landed and taxied to the stern of the ship. Seaplanes are no longer in widespread use in the U.S. Navy; therefore their tenders are no longer needed and most have been inactivated or converted to other missions.

U.S.S. VULCAN (AR-5) *Vulcan* is the lead ship of four sister-ships of the class. These are pre-World War II ships, built between 1938 and 1941. They are 529 feet long, displace 16,200 tons, and have rated speeds of 19.2 knots. They specialize in repair work for all types of ships in the Fleet and may frequently be found in forward areas providing excellent repair service to nearby ships. They carry a crew of 1,100 men, many of them skilled in repair work of different kinds. These auxiliaries are built to fight when necessary—each ship carries four 5-inch guns.

U.S.S. *Vulcan*

U.S.S. APACHE (ATF-67)   Although their arrangements and displacements vary slightly, there are ten Fleet Tugs of the *Apache* class which were built from 1938 to 1940 and are still giving good service. These are the powerful little ships that are called upon for salvage and towing work, and they do an excellent job under sometimes trying conditions. Manned by crews of 85, these 205-foot ships displace only 1,650 tons, yet their diesel engines of 3,000 horsepower can drive the ship at 17 knots, or can tow larger ships off reefs and beaches. They have been known to tow battle-damaged ships thousands of miles to shipyards where the damage could be repaired.

U.S.S. *Repose*

U.S.S. REPOSE (AH-16)   Still another type of auxiliary ship, *Repose* is a floating hospital with the most modern equipment available, including a frozen blood bank—one of eight in existence and the first to be used at sea. The normal capacity of the *Repose* hospital is 560 beds; emergency accommodations for as many as 750 are possible. The hospital staff has a total of 325 persons, including 24 doctors and 3 dentists. Non-medical crew for the ship is 290 men and 19 naval officers. Originally built in 1945, *Repose* was placed in the reserve fleet after World War II. She was recommissioned in 1956 and has provided almost continuous medical service in Vietnam since early 1966, during which time more than 10,000 patients have been cared for. *Repose* is 520 feet long, has a full load displacement of 14,450 tons, and a rated speed of 18 knots.

U.S.S. Vega

U.S.S. VEGA (AF-59)   A refrigerated stores ship, *Vega* is one of the two-ship *Rigel* class. Both ships were built in the mid-1950's from Maritime Administration design adapted to Navy uses. They can follow the Fleet at speeds of 21 knots, keeping up with all but the fastest-moving task forces, ready to provide the fresh and frozen products needed for healthy and happy crews. These ships are 502 feet long and displace 15,450 tons.

U.S.S. PYRO (AE-24)   *Pyro* is an ammunition ship of the five-ship *Suribachi* class. Commissioned in 1959, she is 502 feet long and displaces 17,400 tons with a full load. All of this class have new handling equipment for carrying and transferring guided missiles to the ships using them. They have a rated top speed of 21 knots.

U.S.S. *Pyro*

U.S.S. Hassayampa

U.S.S. HASSAYAMPA (AO-145)
This ship is one of the modern *Neosho* class Fleet Oilers used for underway replenishment of the fuel of those ships that burn oil. There are six sister-ships in this class (AO-143 through AO-148), all built in the 1950 era to the same design. They are 655 feet long, displace 38,000 tons, and have a maximum draft of 35 feet. Their steam turbine main engines produce 28,000 horsepower to drive them at rated speeds of 20 knots. Manned by a crew of 324 officers and men, these ships can each carry 180,000 barrels of fuel oil as cargo.

U.S.S. *Sacramento*

U.S.S. SACRAMENTO (AOE-1)   This is the largest of the auxiliaries: 793 feet long, 39 foot draft, 53,000 tons displacement. Commissioned in 1964, *Sacramento* is the lead ship of a new class which combines the functions of Oiler (AO), Ammunition Ship (AE), and Stores Cargo Ship (AF/AK). She carries 177,000 barrels of oil and aviation fuel, ammunition, and missiles as large as the Talos size. Her two steam turbine main engines produce sufficient power (estimated at 100,000 horsepower) to drive her enormous hull through the water at 26 knots.

Part 8 — SHIPS OF THE FUTURE

Ship designs change as the years go by. Our Navy is constantly looking ahead and designing new ships which will perform their future missions more effectively and more efficiently, no matter what those missions may be. The objectives of new designs are to replace older, obsolete ships and to increase the readiness and effectiveness of the U.S. Navy.

Some new designs are the result of changes in the technology and techniques of warfare. The guided missile ships and the nuclear-powered ships in today's Navy are examples of advancing technology resulting in new ship designs. In earlier years, the development of aircraft led to ships designed to be "aircraft carriers"—as a result, our Fleets of today are strongly oriented toward our carriers and their aircraft.

Some new designs result from changes in mission. The Fleet Ballistic Missile submarine developed from the need for the Navy to assume a new role—that of strategic force for the prevention of enemy attacks. Thus a new mission—strategic deterrent—resulted in perfection of a new type of ship.

Some new designs are developed to combine the missions of several ships into a single hull. The AOE, for example, provides to the operating forces a capability of Oiler, Stores ship, and Ammunition ship all in the same hull.

Finally, some designs are developed simply to take advantage of improvements in certain types of ships, and to improve the new model so it can do the same job better than previous classes.

All of these design changes are important. Whether they will survive through the years or will, in turn, be replaced by still later improvements remains to be seen. Looking ahead, one may visualize the Navy of the future by some of the new ship designs now on the drawing boards and in the minds of the designers. Some of those are shown here. Many of these designs will never be built—they are conceptual; they represent ideas only. Some will be built; others are now being built. These are the artists' conceptions of new designs.

U.S.S. NIMITZ (CVAN-68)
The newest of the nuclear-powered carriers—similar to *Enterprise*. Authorized for construction.

U.S.S. *Nimitz*

GOR 16

U.S.S. *Hudson*

U.S.S. HUDSON (AGOR-16)

The Navy has authorized the construction of a new Oceanographic Research ship of radical new design. The *Hudson* (AGOR-16) (Auxiliary General Oceanographic Research) will be one of two catamaran designs in the shipbuilding program. The catamaran, with her two hulls connected by a large deck structure, provides a great deal more deck space and laboratory space than a conventional ship design—items of great importance to a Research vessel. The *Hudson* will be 246½ feet long, with a beam of 75 feet. Each hull has a 24-foot beam; thus there is 27 feet between hulls. Full load displacement will be 3,080 tons, and cruising speed will be 15 knots. She will have space for a crew of 44 officers and men, and additional accommodations for 25 scientists.

AUXILIARY SUBMARINE RESCUE SHIP (ASR)   This new design is the second catamaran type authorized for construction. Two ships will be built, ASR-21 and ASR-22; they mark the beginning of a new class to replace the ten present ASRs which have been in the Fleet for more than 20 years. ASRs have as their mission the salvage and rescue of submarines. The new class of ASR will be able to provide services of all types to rescue operations of submarines, and, in addition, will be able to support the new Deep Submergence Rescue Vehicle (DSRV) which will provide improved rescue capability over that presently available. The new ASR class will be 251 feet long, and will have a beam of 86 feet. Full load displacement will be 3,400 tons. The ship's complement will be six officers and 109 enlisted men. She will have a rated speed of 15 knots for sustained operations. Since the DSRVs are 50 feet long, weigh 125,000 pounds, and carry a crew of three, the problem of handling aboard an ASR was recognized as a major one. With the catamaran design of new ASRs, the rescue vehicle can be launched and recovered between the two hulls.

AMPHIBIOUS ASSAULT SHIP (LHA) A two-year Navy study demonstrated that a multipurpose amphibious force ship would be an effective successor to previous types of amphibious ships and reduce the requirement for specialized ship types. The LHA will be a new class to meet the requirements of the multipurpose ship. It is designed to combine the features of the amphibious assault ship (LPH), the amphibious transport dock (LPD), the attack cargo ship (LKA), and the dock landing ship (LSD). The LHA will have a full flight deck for helicopters and well deck for landing craft, and will carry a balanced assault payload. Principal characteristics are: length, 796 feet; beam, 106 feet; and speed rated at more than 20 knots. This LHA is expected to be adaptable to changing amphibious doctrine during the next thirty years, and to be able to perform the entire range of possible combat missions.

FAST DEPLOYMENT LOGISTIC SHIP (FDL)   The FDL is a proposed new class of ship which would carry quantities of heavy combat equipment and initial combat supplies for landing forces. Its mission would be to deploy large, fully equipped landing forces to any of a great many places in the world on schedules much faster than anything heretofore attained. The loaded ships could be located at sea near potential trouble areas. If U.S. forces were required in the area, the equipment on the ships would be offloaded over-the-beach or in a friendly port. A major objective is to reduce to a minimum the time required to respond to aggression.

INDEX

2812-11A
52